Bilingual

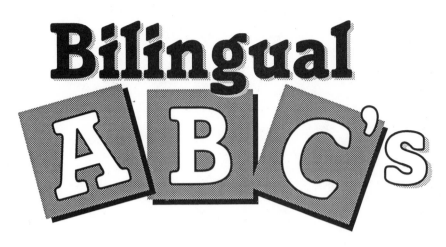

A Spanish-English Alphabet Book

by Nancy McColl and Karen Paskowitz

Fearon Teacher Aids
An imprint of Paramount Supplemental Education

Editorial Director: Virginia L. Murphy

Editor: Carolea Williams

Copyeditor: Christine Hood

Cover and Inside Design: Good Neighbor Press, Inc., Grand Junction, CO

Inside Illustration: Jackie Urbanovic

ISBN 0-86653-904-2

Printed in the United States of America

1. 9 8 7 6 5 4 3 2 1

Contents

Introduction

Bilingual ABC's provides you with unique and exciting ways to build a strong reading readiness foundation with your students. Two simple art projects are presented for each letter of the alphabet. Each art activity illustrates a word that begins with the same letter in both Spanish and English. The materials can be used in a bilingual Spanish-English classroom, a mono-lingual classroom of either language, or in an ESL program. Each project helps children develop letter and sound recognition, fine motor skills, listening skills, and creative expression.

Some adjustments have been made to accommodate the differences between Spanish and English. For example, there are no words in Spanish that begin with the letter K or W. Therefore, pairs of words for these letters will not match exactly. Also, a few non-standard but commonly used and accepted Spanish words have been included.

The projects have been designed using materials readily available in your classroom. Few patterns are used. For example, children are asked to round the corners of a square to make a circle rather than trace a circle pattern. In addition to the art projects, several letter activity ideas are included that can be integrated across the curriculum.

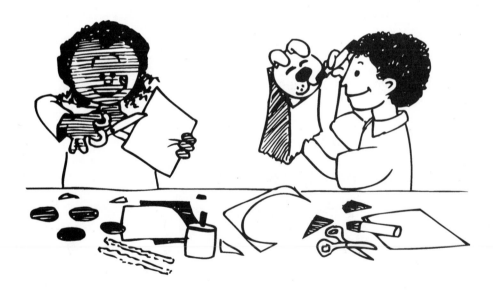

crobat • El Acróbata

Materials (for each child)

- aluminum foil
  two 1 1/2" x 8" (3.75 cm x 20 cm) strips for arms and legs
  3" x 4" (7.5 cm x 10 cm) strip for body
  3" (7.5 cm) square for head
- two drinking straws
- 24" (60 cm) piece of yarn or string
- two 1" (2.5 cm) strips of tape

Directions

1. Roll the foil for the arms, legs, and body between your palms to make long, thin pieces.

2. Wrap the arm and leg pieces around the body in the appropriate places.

3. Roll the 3" (7.5 cm) square piece of foil into a ball for the head.

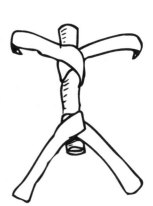

4. Press the head firmly onto the body.

5. String the yarn through the two drinking straws.

6. Tape each end of the yarn to the end of a straw.

7. Hang the acrobat on the "high wire" by bending the ends of the arms over the yarn between the two straws.

8. Encourage children to hold a straw in each hand and make the acrobat flip around the yarn.

Follow-Up Activities

Acrobatic Stunts

Encourage children to try some simple acrobatic stunts on mats or a grassy play area. Children can try doing a somersault, walking a tight rope placed on the ground, or doing a cartwheel. Be sure to monitor students closely and ensure their safety.

A-OK

Invite students to brainstorm a list of occupations or trades that begin with the letter A. Your list might include actress (la actriz), actor (el actor), architect (la arquitecta), astronomer (el astrónomo), athlete (el atleta), archer (el arquero), artist (la artista), and astronaut (el astronauta).

All About Acrobats

Read *I Am Jesse White, Tumbler* by Diane Schmidt (Niles, Illinois: Whitman, 1990). This story tells of a young boy who participates in a competitive tumbling team in Chicago. The text is complemented by actual photographs.

irplane • El Avión

Materials (for each child)

- airplane pattern on page 110 reproduced on heavy white stock
- 12" (30 cm) piece of yarn or roving
- two pieces of clear tape
- crayons or markers
- hole punch
- scissors

Directions

1. Cut out the airplane body and wing.

2. Using crayons or markers, draw windows and people on the airplane.

3. Cut along the dotted line using scissors or an X-acto knife (teacher use only) to create a slit for the wing.

4. Insert the wing through the slit in the airplane body.

5. Using tape, secure the wing in place on each side.

6. Punch a hole in the nose of the airplane and tie the yarn through the hole.

Follow-Up Activities

Adventure Awaits

Encourage children to arrange chairs or outdoor blocks to create the inside of an airplane. Invite children to pretend they are flying to an adventurous land. Some children can pretend to be passengers and others can be crew members.

Airport Action

Provide children with a large sheet of butcher paper to create an airport runway for their airplanes. Encourage children to use crayons and markers to draw details.

All About Airplanes

Read *First Flight* by David McPhail (Boston: Little Brown, 1987). In this story, a naughty teddy bear goes on a trip with his owner. By ignoring the rules, he disrupts their first airplane adventure.

Beard • La Barba

Materials (for each child)

- ten 1" x 12" (2.5 cm x 30 cm) strips of construction paper (brown, black, gray, orange, white, or yellow)
- 1 yard (1 m) of roving (same color as paper)
- glue
- pencil

Directions

1. Roll each strip of paper around a pencil to curl it.

2. Fold down a 1" (2.5 cm) flap on one end of each strip.

3. Glue the flaps over the roving in the center to cover a 10" (25 cm) section.

4. When the glue is dry, place the beard under a child's chin and tie the roving on top of his or her head.

Follow-Up Activities

Beard Colors

Make a graph to represent the colors children chose to make their beards. Encourage children to interpret the graph results by asking questions such as "Which color was used most often?" "How many children made black beards?" "Which color was used the least?"

Barber Shop

Encourage children to set up a barber and/or beauty shop in the dramatic play section of the classroom. Include mirrors, empty shampoo bottles, towels, hairbrushes, and combs. Invite children to groom their beards and style their hair.

Bundle of Beards

Provide magazines and invite children to find and cut out pictures of people with beards. Display the pictures on a chart or bulletin board. Encourage children to make a list of words that describe the beards. Write the descriptive words next to the appropriate pictures.

Boat and Whale
• El Barco y La Ballena

Materials (for each child)

- construction paper
  4" x 18" (10 cm x 45 cm) blue for water
  3" x 5" (7.5 cm x 12.5 cm) brown for boat
  4" (10 cm) white square for sail
  6" x 9" (15 cm x 22.5 cm) black for whale
- 6" (15 cm) popsicle stick or pipe cleaner for mast
- two 3" x 5" (7.5 cm x 12.5 cm) strips of white tissue paper for water spray
- two brass fasteners
- glue
- scissors

Directions

1. Tear along one long edge of the 4" x 18" (10 cm x 45 cm) piece of blue construction paper to make water waves.

2. Using scissors, round off the two bottom corners of the 3" x 5" (7.5 cm x 12.5 cm) piece of brown construction paper to make the boat.

3. Fold the 4" (10 cm) white square in half to locate the center along one edge. Cut from the two lower corners up to the center fold to make a triangle sail.

4. Glue the sail to the pipe cleaner mast and attach it to the boat.

5. Cut the 6" x 9" (15 cm x 22.5 cm) piece of black construction paper into the shape of a whale.

6. Using scissors, fringe the two white strips of tissue paper.

7. Glue the white tissue fringe to the top of the whale to represent water spraying from the blow hole.

8. Fasten the bottom of the boat and the bottom of the whale to the top of the waves using the brass fasteners.

Follow-Up Activities

B oat Regatta

Give each child a cardboard box big enough to sit in. Invite each child to decorate the cardboard box so it looks like a boat. Encourage children to sit in their boats and pretend to row as the class sings, "Row, Row, Row Your Boat."

B oat Float

Read *The Boats on a River* by Marjorie Flack (New York: Viking Press, 1991). This is an attractive book for young children that includes pictures of a variety of boats including ferry boats, tug boats, and ocean liners.

B etween Friends

Read *Amos and Boris* by William Steig (New York: Crowell, 1971). In this story, a mouse and a whale are surprised to discover that they share many things in common, including the fact that they are both mammals.

C ar • El Coche

Materials (for each child)

- construction paper
  6" x 12" (15 cm x 30 cm) any color for car body
  4 1/2" x 8" (11.25 cm x 20 cm) any color for car top
  two 4" (10 cm) black squares for tires
  3" x 6" (7.5 cm x 15 cm) white for window
- aluminum foil
  two 2" (5 cm) squares for hubcaps
  scraps for bumper and door handles
- red and yellow tissue paper scraps for lights
- scissors
- glue
- crayons or markers

Directions

1. Round off all corners of the 6" x 12" (15 cm x 30 cm) piece of construction paper to make the body of the car.

2. Round off two corners of the 4 1/2" x 8" (11.25 cm x 20 cm) piece of construction paper to make the top of the car.

3. Glue the top of the car to the body of the car.

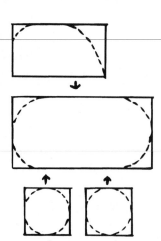

4. Round off all corners of the two 4" (10 cm) squares of black construction paper to make the car tires.

5. Glue the tires to the car.

6. Round off the corners of the 3" x 6" (7.5 cm x 15 cm) piece of white construction paper to make the window.

7. Glue the window to the top half of the car.

8. Round off all corners of the two 2" (5 cm) square pieces of foil to make the hubcaps.

9. Glue the hubcaps to the tires.

10. Use foil scraps to add bumpers to the front and back of the car.

11. Add yellow tissue puffs to the front of the car and the red tissue puffs to the back to make lights.

12. Using crayons or markers, draw a door and the driver in the car.

Follow-Up Activities

Car Colors

Discuss the color of cars owned by the children's families. Make a graph representing these colors. Invite children to intrepret the information on the graph by asking them questions such as, "Which color of car is most popular?" "How many families own blue cars?"

Cars, Cars, Cars

Read *Cars* by Anne Rockwell (New York: E.P. Dutton, 1984). This simple book explores everything from racing cars to limousines including the speed at which they travel and where they go. Ask students what type of car they would like to own and why.

Car Collections

Invite children to bring toy cars to school. Talk about the cars and sort them by various attributes such as size and color.

Castle • El Castillo

Materials (for each child)

- construction paper
  two 3" x 12" (7.5 cm x 30 cm) gray for towers
  9" x 12" (22.5 cm x 30 cm) gray for castle
  4" (10 cm) brown square for drawbridge
  four 1 1/2" x 2" (3.75 cm x 5 cm) various bright colors for flags
- four toothpicks
- crayons or markers
- scissors
- glue

Directions

1. Cut points on one 3" (7.5 cm) end of both 3" x 12" (7.5 cm x 30 cm) gray pieces of construction paper to make towers.

2. Glue the towers to each 9" (22.5 cm) edge of the 9" x 12" (22.5 cm x 30 cm) castle.

3. Make a 1/2" (1.25 cm) fold along one edge of the 4" (10 cm) square of brown construction paper to make the drawbridge.

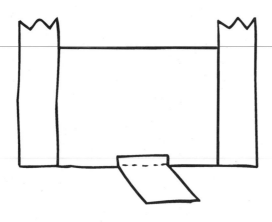

4. Glue the folded flap of the drawbridge to the center bottom edge of the castle so the drawbridge opens down.

5. Fold the drawbridge up. Using a black crayon or marker, trace around the edge of drawbridge to make its outline on the front of the castle.

6. Fold the drawbridge down. Using crayons or markers, draw a king and queen in the outlined space.

7. Glue each 1 1/2" x 2" (3.75 cm x 5 cm) brightly-colored flag to a toothpick.

8. Glue the flags to the top of the castle towers.

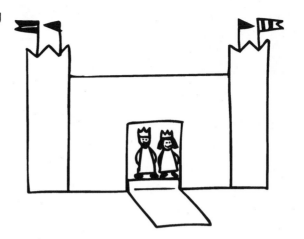

Follow-Up Activities

Castle Construction

Encourage children to use floor blocks to build castles in the dramatic play center. Children can pretend to be a king (el rey), queen (la reina), princess (la princesa), or prince (el príncipe) as they sit on the throne (el trono) or cross the drawbridge (el puente levadizo).

Creative Capers

Encourage children to brainstorm ways to complete this sentence: "If I were king or queen of the castle, I would . . . ." Invite children to draw pictures to represent their ideas. Add dictation to the bottom of each picture as children describe their illustrations. Bind the pictures together to make a class book.

Castle Characters

Read the book *May I Bring a Friend?* by Beatrice Schenk DeRegniers (New York: Atheneum, 1964). In this delightful story, a young boy visits the King and Queen each day of the week. Each day he invites different friends to join him and come along.

inosaur • El Dinosaurio

Materials (for each child)

- construction paper
  12" x 18" (30 cm x 45 cm) any color for background
  9" x 12" (22.5 cm x 30 cm) gray, brown, or green for dinosaur
- crayons or markers
- scissors
- glue

Directions

1. Round off the corners of the 9" x 12" (22.5 cm x 30 cm) gray, brown, or green piece of construction paper to make a dinosaur body.

2. Glue the body to the 12" x 18" (30 cm x 45 cm) background.

3. Using crayons or markers, add details to the dinosaur picture.

4. Write the word *dinosaur* or *el dinosaurio* on the picture.

Follow-Up Activities

Days Gone By

Remind students that while no one living today has ever seen a real dinosaur, scientists know they existed because of the fossils found in archeological explorations. Invite students to make their own fossil prints. Collect leaves and press them into clay. Allow the clay to harden. Brush away the dried leaves to reveal the prints left in the hardened clay.

Danny and the Dinosaur

Read Syd Hoff's *Danny and the Dinosaur* (New York: Harper & Row, 1958). This is the story of Danny's unforgettable day in the city with a museum dinosaur. The book is also available in Spanish—*Danielito y el Dinosaurio*.

Dinosaur Data

Encourage children to share what they know about dinosaurs and then share some new dinosaur data with students. For example, ask students if they know that there were thousands of different kinds of dinosaurs, that dinosaur fossils have been found on every continent except Antarctica, and that not all dinosaurs were large. The Saltopus was about the size of a chicken.

Doctor • El Doctor(a)

Materials (for each child)

- construction paper
  2" x 24" (5 cm x 60 cm) white for headband
  12" x 18" (30 cm x 45 cm) black for medical bag
  two 4 1/2" x 6" (11.25 cm x 15 cm) black for bag handles
  four 2" x 6" (5 cm x 15 cm) red for cross
- 3" (7.5 cm) tagboard circle
- 4" (10 cm) square aluminum foil
- scissors
- glue
- stapler

Directions

1. Spread glue on one side of the 3" (7.5 cm) tagboard circle and cover it with the 4" (10 cm) square of aluminum foil. Wrap the foil around the edges of the circle.

2. Glue the foil circle to the center of the 2" x 24" (5 cm x 60 cm) white headband.

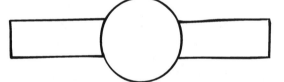

3. Staple the headband to fit around each child's head.

4. To make the medical bag, fold each 18" (45 cm) edge of the 12" x 18" (30 cm x 45 cm) black construction paper over 1" (2.5 cm).

5. Spread glue on both 1" (2.5 cm) flaps.

6. Fold the paper in half (folded edges inside) to form a 9" x 10" (22.5 cm x 25 cm) bag.

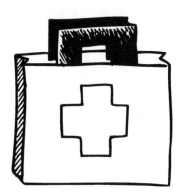

7. Place the two 4 1/2" x 6" (11.25 cm x 15 cm) black rectangles together and cut a 3" x 4" (7.5 cm x 10 cm) rectangle from the center of one lower edge to make two handles.

8. Glue the handles inside of the bag.

9. Glue two 2" x 6" (5 cm x 15 cm) red pieces of construction paper on each side of the bag to make red crosses.

Follow-Up Activities

Dodging Disease

Invite the school nurse to visit the class and talk about good health habits. Remind children of simple ways to reduce the spread of germs, such as covering their mouths when coughing or sneezing and washing their hands frequently.

Doctors Don't Do It All

Read the book *Ouch! A Book About Cuts, Scratches and Scrapes* by Melvin Berger (New York: Lodestar Books, 1991). This simple book provides easily understood explanations of how the body works to repair itself after a cut or scrape.

Doctor's Duties

Practice simple first aid procedures such as washing small cuts and covering them with a band-aid.

Elephant • El Elefante

Materials (for each child)

- construction paper
  9" (22.5 cm) gray square for head
  two 6" x 8" (15 cm x 20 cm) gray for ears
  2" x 8" (5 cm x 20 cm) gray for trunk
  two 1" x 2" (2.5 cm x 5 cm) brown for eyes/eyelashes
  two 1" x 6" (2.5 cm x 15 cm) white for tusks
- brass fastener
- scissors
- pencil
- glue
- crayons or markers

Directions

1. Round off the corners of the 9" (22.5 cm) square gray head.

2. Round off the corners on one side of each 6" x 8" (15 cm x 20 cm) gray piece of construction paper to make two ears.

3. Glue an ear to the back of each side of the head.

4. Fold the ears forward.

5. Fringe one long edge of each 1" x 2" (2.5 cm x 5 cm) piece of brown construction paper to make eyelashes.

6. Curl the fringe around a pencil.

7. Glue the two fringed eyes on the head with the lashes curling upward.

8. Draw wrinkles on the 2" x 8" (5 cm x 20 cm) gray trunk.

9. Fasten the trunk to the head with a brass fastener.

10. Curl the trunk around a pencil.

11. Cut one end of each 1" x 6" (2.5 cm x 15 cm) white tusk to make points.

12. Glue the tusks on each side of the trunk.

Follow-Up Activities

Elephant Walk

Invite children to do the "elephant walk" by walking very slowly with heavy steps. Encourage children to clasp their hands in front of their bodies to make an elephant trunk. Show children how to swing their trunks from side to side as they walk. Play some appropriate music to set the mood.

Elephant Moon

Read *Elephant Moon* by Bijou Le Tord (New York: Doubleday, 1993). The story takes place on the plains of eastern Africa where small herds of African elephants live. The story's text and beautiful watercolor illustrations pay tribute to these grand creatures who are disappearing from our earth.

Enormous Elephant Facts

Test student knowledge of elephants by asking them to vote *yes* or *no* to the following true/false statements.

There are two kinds of elephants. (True, African and Asiatic)
Elephants are the largest animals that live on land. (True)
A newborn baby elephant weighs 60 pounds. (False, 200 pounds)
Elephants love water and take baths often. (True)

Exercise • El Ejercicio

Materials (for each child)

- construction paper (any color)
  4" (10 cm) square for head
  4" x 6" (10 cm x 15 cm) for body
  two 2" x 6" (5 cm x 15 cm) for arms
  two 2" x 8" (5 cm x 20 cm) for legs
- four brass fasteners
- four 6" (15 cm) pieces of string or yarn
- crayons or markers
- scissors
- glue

Directions

1. Round off all corners of the 4" (10 cm) square of construction paper to make the head.

2. Round off all corners of the 4" x 6" (10 cm x 15 cm) piece of construction paper to make the body.

3. Glue the head to the top of the body.

4. Using crayons or markers, draw a face.

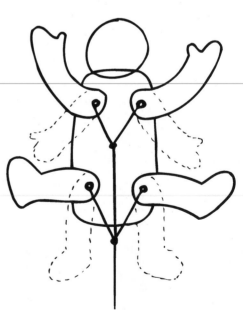

5. Round off all corners of the 2" x 6" (5 cm x 15 cm) and 2" x 8" (5 cm x 20 cm) pieces of construction paper to make arms and legs.

6. Attach the arms and legs to the body using brass fasteners.

7. Using one 6" (15 cm) piece of string, connect the two arm brass fasteners.

8. Using another piece of string, connect the two leg brass fasteners.

9. Tie a third piece of string to the center of the string between the arms and the center of the string between the legs.

10. Tie one end of the fourth string to the string between the legs and allow the string to hang down.

11. Show children how to pull on the last string to cause the arms and legs of the exerciser to fly up.

Follow-Up Activities

Everybody Exercises

Show children a simple routine of exercises that they can do every day. The routine might include jumping jacks, windmills, toe touches, and running in place.

Exercise Improvement

Help each child choose one exercise they would like to repeat every day at home for a month. Ask children to record how many repetitions of the exercise they do each day. When the month-long records are completed, encourage children to interpret their data. For example, were children able to do more repetitions as time went by?

Exercise Book

Invite children to draw a picture of themselves exercising. Help children complete the following sentence at the bottom of their illustration, "My favorite exercise is . . . ." Combine the pages to make a class exercise book.

Flowers • **Las Flores**

Materials (for each child)

- tissue paper
  three 3" (7.5 cm) red squares for flower
  three 3" (7.5 cm) yellow squares for flower
  three 3" (7.5 cm) orange squares for flower
  six 2" x 3" (5 cm x 7.5 cm) green for leaves
- three 6" (15 cm) green pipe cleaners
- styrofoam cup
- scissors
- glue

Directions

1. Round off all corners of the 3" (7.5 cm) squares of red, yellow, and orange tissue to make flower circles.

2. String each set of same-colored circles on a separate pipe cleaner.

3. Bend the end of the pipe cleaner in the center of each flower.

4. Cut off the corners of each 2" x 3" (5 cm x 7.5 cm) piece of green tissue to make leaves.

5. Wrap two green leaves around each pipe cleaner and secure them in place with glue.

6. Poke each pipe cleaner stem through the bottom of an upside-down styrofoam cup.

Follow-Up Activities

F **eed the Flowers**

Help children plant flower seeds in cups or cans filled with potting soil. Show children how to water and care for the seedlings as they grow.

F **lower Garden**

Read *Planting a Rainbow* by Lois Ehlert (San Diego: Harcourt Brace Jovanovich, 1988). In this story, beautiful and bold illustrations feature a mother and child planting a rainbow of colorful blooms.

F **antastic Flower Garden**

Invite children to paint large flowers on construction paper using bright colors of tempera paint. After the paintings dry, help children cut out their flowers. Display the colorful blooms on a bulletin board to create a fantastic flower garden.

ruit • La Fruta

Materials (for each child)

- construction paper
  4 1/2" x 12" (11.25 cm x 30 cm) brown for bowl
  9" x 12" (22.5 cm x 30 cm) blue for background
  3" (7.5 cm) orange square for orange
  3" (7.5 cm) red square for apple
  3" (7.5 cm) light green square for apple
  2" x 6" (5 cm x 15 cm) yellow for banana
  1" x 10" (2.5 cm x 25 cm) light green or purple for grapes
  4" x 6" (10 cm x 15 cm) dark green for leaves
- crayons or markers
- scissors
- glue

Directions

1. Round off the bottom two corners of the brown construction paper to make a bowl.

2. Round off the corners of the orange, red, and light green squares to make an orange and two apples.

3. Trim the yellow construction paper to look like a banana.

4. Glue the fruit in the bowl.

5. Cut the 1" x 10" (2.5 cm x 25 cm) strip of light green or purple construction paper into ten 1" (2.5 cm) squares.

6. Round off the corners of each square to make grapes.

7. Glue four grapes in a row on the background paper. Glue three grapes in a row below the first row. Add a row of two grapes, and then finally glue the last grape underneath the other rows.

8. Cut the dark green construction paper into leaves and glue in appropriate places on the fruit.

9. Glue the bowl of fruit to the blue background. Use crayons or markers to add details.

Follow-Up Activities

Friendship Fruit Salad

Invite each child to bring a piece of his or her favorite fruit to class. Help children cut the fruit into bite-sized pieces and combine them to make a friendship fruit salad.

Fruit Basket Upset

Invite children to sit in chairs in a circle. Choose four fruit names and assign each child one name. Take away one chair and ask the child without the chair to stand in the center of the circle. Invite the standing child to call out the name of one of the four fruits. Each child with that fruit name must stand and find a new chair. Meanwhile, the child in the center tries to find an empty chair to sit in. The child left without a chair stands in the center and calls out a fruit name as the game continues. If a child calls out "fruit basket upset," every child must find a new chair.

Favorite Fruit Graph

Provide an assortment of magazines or newspaper ads. Invite each child to cut out a picture of his or her favorite fruit. Place the fruit pictures in horizontal or vertical lines to create a graph.

arage • El Garaje

Materials (for each child)

- construction paper
  3" x 12" (7.5 cm x 30 cm) any color for garage
  3" x 4" (7.5 cm x 10 cm) any color for car
- small milk carton (top cut off)
- crayons or markers
- scissors
- glue

Directions

1. Fold the 3" x 12" (7.5 cm x 30 cm) strip of construction paper around the milk carton so the ends overlap. Glue it in place.

2. Tip the carton upside down so the bottom becomes the roof of the garage.

3. Make the garage door by cutting two slits on one side of the carton.

4. Fold the flap up to open the door.

5. Fold the 3" x 4" (7.5 cm x 10 cm) piece of construction paper in half to make a 3" x 2" (7.5 cm x 5 cm) piece of paper.

6. Draw a car on the folded paper so the top of the car is along the fold.

7. Cut out the car but do not cut on the fold.

8. Using crayons or markers, add details to the car (doors, wheels, driver).

9. Invite children to open the door to the garage and "drive" the car inside.

Follow-Up Activities

Garage Sale

Play a verbal memory game. The first child says, "In my garage, I have a (blank)." The next child repeats the sentence and then adds another garage sale item. The third child repeats what the two children previously have said and adds a third item. The game continues with the garage sale list getting longer and longer. Pictures of the garage sale objects will be especially helpful for ESL students.

Garage Goodies

Create a display of tools commonly found in a garage such as pliers, screwdriver, hammer, saw, wrench, and nails. Teach children the name of each tool and talk about how it is used.

Guess the Tool

After children have learned the names of common tools, play a memory game. Display all the tools and give children a chance to carefully look them over. Place a towel over the tool display and remove one of the objects. Uncover the display and challenge children to name the missing tool.

 **oose • El Ganso**

Materials (for each child)

- construction paper
  6" (15 cm) white square for head
  4" x 9" (10 cm x 22.5 cm) yellow for bill
  two 4" x 6" (10 cm x 15 cm) white for wings
- white paper bag
- crayons or markers
- scissors
- glue

Directions

1. Round off all corners of the white square to make the head.

2. Glue the head to the bottom flap of the white paper bag.

3. Fold the yellow construction paper in half to become 4" x 4 1/2" (10 cm x 11.25 cm).

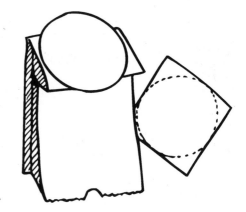

4. Round off two corners of folded yellow construction paper to make the bill.

5. Glue the bill to the bottom of the head.

6. Round off one corner of each 4" x 6" (10 cm x 15 cm) white piece of construction paper to make wings.

7. Glue the wings to the sides of the paper bag.

8. Add details using crayons or markers.

Follow-Up Activities

Goose Game

Play the circle game, "Duck, Duck, Goose." Invite children to sit in a circle. "It" walks around the outside of the circle touching the head of each child and saying, "duck" with each tap. Finally, "it" says "goose" as he or she taps a child's head. That child chases "it" around the circle. If "it" makes it all the way around the circle without being caught, the child who was chasing becomes the new "it."

Gaggle of Geese

A flock of geese when not in flight is called a gaggle. Ask children if they know any other names for animal groups. For example, a company of lions is called a pride, a group of cows is called a herd, a cluster of seals is called a pod, and fish travel in schools.

Gander or Gosling?

Share some interesting facts about geese with children. For example, a male goose is called a gander and a baby goose is a gosling. Geese build their nests in the grass. Geese fly together in a V formation.

 ello • Hola

Materials (for each child)

- construction paper
  9" (22.5 cm) pink or brown square for head
  4 1/2" x 12" (11.25 cm x 30 cm) any color for shirt shoulders
  6" (15 cm) pink or brown square for hand
  two 3" x 6" (7.5 cm x 15 cm) same color as shirt for sleeve
  4 1/2" x 6" (11.25 cm x 15 cm) white for word balloon
- brass fastener
- crayons or markers
- scissors
- glue

Directions

1. Round off all corners of the 9" (22.5 cm) square of pink or brown construction paper to make a head.

2. Round off the top two corners of the 4 1/2" x 12" (11.25 cm x 30 cm) piece of construction paper to make the shoulders.

3. Glue the head to the shoulders.

4. Using crayons or markers, add facial features.

5. Trace around your hand on the 6" (15 cm) square of pink or brown construction paper and cut it out.

6. Glue the hand to the end of one 3" x 6" (7.5 cm x 15 cm) piece of construction paper.

7. Using a brass fastener, connect this piece to the other 3" x 6" (7.5 cm x 15 cm) piece to make a bent elbow.

8. Glue the arm to the shoulder.

9. Round off three corners of the 4 1/2" x 6" (11.25 cm x 15 cm) piece of white construction paper.

10. Write the word *hello*, *hi*, or *hola* on the white word balloon.

11. Glue the word balloon next to the face with the pointed end closest to the mouth.

Follow-Up Activities

**ello Around the World**

Learn to say hello in several different languages.

Hola (Spanish)
Neé how (Chinese)
Ohío (Japanese)
Borév (Armenian)
Bon jour (French)
Guten tag (German)
On yúng (Korean)

ello, How Are You?

Encourage children to practice greeting their classmates and those they meet in the hallway or on the playground.

ello, Amigos!

Read *Hello, Amigos!* by Tricia Brown (New York: Holt, 1986). In this story, a young boy tells of his day at school as he celebrates his birthday. The text includes many Spanish words and cultural information.

Hippopotamus
• El Hipopótamo

Materials (for each child)

- construction paper
  12" (30 cm) brown square for body
  8" x 16" (20 cm x 40 cm) brown for head
  two 2" (5 cm) brown squares for ears
  two 1" x 2" (2.5 cm x 5 cm) brown for eyelids
  3" (7.5 cm) pink square for tongue
  1" x 4" (2.5 cm x 10 cm) white for teeth
  two 3" (7.5 cm) brown squares for legs

- black crayon or marker
- pencil
- scissors
- glue

Directions

1. Round off the corners of the 12" (30 cm) square of brown construction paper to make the body.

2. Fold the 8" x 16" (20 cm x 40 cm) piece of brown construction paper in half to make an 8" (20 cm) square. The folded edge will be the top of the head.

3. Round off the corners of the folded paper making the top of the head narrower than the bottom. Glue the head to the center of the body with the folded edge at the top.

4. Round off all corners of the two 2" (5 cm) squares of brown construction paper to make the ears. Glue the ears to the top of the head.

5. Round off all corners of the two 1" x 2" (2.5 cm x 5 cm) pieces of brown construction paper to make eyelids.

6. Fringe one long edge of each eyelid to make eyelashes. Glue the eyelids to the head and curl the eyelashes upward by wrapping them around a pencil.

7. Using a black crayon or marker, draw eyes below the eyelids and draw two nostrils in the appropriate place.

8. Round off two corners of the 3" (7.5 cm) square of pink construction paper to make the tongue.

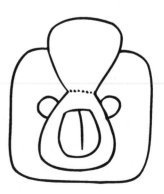

9. Open the top layer of the head and glue the tongue inside the mouth.

10. Cut the 1" x 4" (2.5 cm x 10 cm) white strip of construction paper into 1" (2.5 cm) squares to make four teeth.

11. Make a flap on each tooth by folding over one edge and glue the flap of each tooth inside the mouth. Glue one tooth on each side of the upper jaw and one tooth on each side of the lower jaw.

12. Round the corners of the two 3" (7.5 cm) squares of brown construction paper to make the legs and glue them to the bottom of the hippo.

Follow-Up Activities

Hippo Habitat

Share some interesting facts with children about hippos and the places they live. Hippos like to be in the water. Their eyes, ears, and nostrils are on top of their head so they can see and breathe even when they are almost completely covered with water. Hippos live in rivers, lakes, and streams in Africa and they eat grasses and water plants.

Hippos in Literature

Read *George and Martha* by James Marshall (Boston: Houghton Mifflin, 1972). This book is a compilation of five short stories that center around two great hippo friends that solve life's daily problems.

Huge Hippos

Invite children to speculate how big a hippopotamus is. Using chalk, draw the outline of a hippo on the play yard. (Hippos can be 12-15 feet [3.5-4.5 m] long, are about three feet [1 m] tall, and are barrel-shaped.) Find out how many children can stand inside the hippo outline. Total the weight of the children standing on the hippo. Compare this sum to the weight of a hippo (5,000-8,000 pounds).

nsect • El Insecto

Materials (for each child)

- three connected sections of an egg carton for body
- eight 3" (7.5 cm) pipe cleaners for legs
- construction paper scraps for wings
- tempera paint
- paintbrushes
- glue
- crayons or markers

Directions

1. Paint the egg carton sections so it looks like an insect body.

2. After the paint is dry, add three pipe cleaners to each side of the insect's body by sticking them into the egg carton.

3. Place the other two pipe cleaners on the front section to represent antennae.

4. Use scraps of paper to make wings. Glue them in place.

5. Add other details using crayons or markers.

Follow-Up Activities

Insects Here and There

Create a bulletin board display using the insects the children have made. Cover the bulletin board with blue background paper. Add long green strips along the bottom and place a bright sun in the sky. Add the insects in the grass and flying overhead.

Insects in the Garden

Read Dorothy Souza's book *Insects in the Garden* (Minneapolis: Carolrhoda, 1991). This book describes the life cycle and habits of various insects found in a common garden.

Insect Inspection

Invite children to look for insects at home or at school. Challenge them to notice the ways the insects are different or the same. If possible, set up an ant farm in the classroom. This is a fascinating way to study how involved the lives of insects can be.

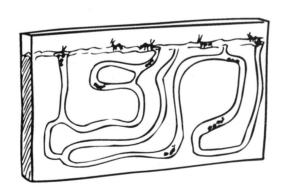

I sland • La Isla

Materials (for each child)

- construction paper
  6" x 9" (15 cm x 22.5 cm) dark brown for island
  12" x 18" (30 cm x 45 cm) blue for background
  4" (10 cm) brown square for tree trunks
  4" (10 cm) green square for palm fronds
  2" (5 cm) yellow square for sun
- white chalk
- glue

Directions

1. Tear the edges of the 6" x 9" (15 cm x 22.5 cm) piece of dark brown construction paper to make an island.

2. Glue the island to the center of the blue background.

3. Tear the brown square into two strips to make tree trunks.

4. Glue the tree trunks to the island.

5. Tear the green square into narrow strips to make palm fronds.

6. Glue the palm fronds to the tops of the trees.

7. Use the scraps of brown construction paper to tear coconut shapes.

8. Glue the coconuts in the palm trees.

9. Tear the corners of the yellow square to make a round sun.

10. Glue the sun in the sky.

11. Using white chalk, draw waves on the water.

12. Using white chalk, write *island* or *la isla*.

Follow-Up Activities

Island Hula

Encourage children to learn the hula. Hula dancers gently swing their hips and use their hands to tell a story. Hands can make movements to indicate the motion of waves or trees blowing in the wind.

Island Visit

Read *My Little Island* by Frané Lessac (New York: Harper & Row, 1984). In this story, a young boy returns with his best friend Lucca to the Caribbean island where he was born. Together the boys experience tropical fruits, huge iguanas, calypso music, and many other wonders of island life.

Island Hunt

Using a globe or map of the world, challenge children to locate islands around the world. Discuss what an island is and what makes it special.

J elly • La Jalea

Materials (for each child)

- construction paper
  6" x 9" (15 cm x 22.5 cm) white for jar
  2" x 3" (5 cm x 7.5 cm) white for label
- 1" (2.5 cm) purple tissue paper squares for jelly
- 1" x 4" (2.5 cm x 10 cm) strip aluminum foil for lid
- liquid starch
- paintbrush
- scissors
- glue

Directions

1. Round off all corners of the bottom of the 6" x 9" (15 cm x 22.5 cm) piece of white construction paper to make a jar. Cut a curved neck shape at the top of the jar.

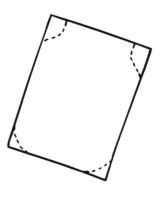

2. Fill the jar with jelly by painting liquid starch on the paper and layering it with squares of purple tissue paper.

3. Glue the foil to the top of the jar to make a lid.

4. Write the word *jelly* or *la jalea* on the 2" x 3" (5 cm x 7.5 cm) piece of white construction paper to make a label.

5. Glue the label to the jar.

Follow-Up Activities

Jelly Tasting

Provide children with several flavors of jelly and a supply of crackers on which to spread it. Invite children to have a jelly tasting party.

Jelly Bean Probability

Fill a paper bag with two colors of jelly beans. Invite each child to reach into the bag and take two jelly beans out. Before children open their hand to see what color the jelly beans are, ask them to guess if they think the jelly beans will be the same color or two different colors. Make a graph to show how many children got two jelly beans the same color and how many got two jelly beans of different colors.

Jolly Jam and Jelly Books

Bruce Degen's *Jamberry* (New York: Harper & Row, 1983) is a rhyming story that takes children through a berry world. Russell Hoban's *Bread and Jam for Frances* (New York: Harper & Row, 1964) is a book children will identify with as Frances expresses her desire to eat only her favorite food—bread and jam.

ewels • Las Joyas

Materials (for each child)

- construction paper
  4" x 9" (10 cm x 22.5 cm) brown for treasure chest lid
  8" x 9" (20 cm x 22.5 cm) brown for treasure chest
- twenty 1 1/2" (3.75 cm) various colored squares of tissue for jewels
- scraps of aluminum foil for silver treasures
- sequins and glitter
- brass fastener
- glue
- scissors

Directions

1. Round off two corners along the 9" (22.5 cm) edge of the 4" x 9" (10 cm x 22.5 cm) piece of brown construction paper to make the treasure chest lid.

2. Place the lid on top of the 8" x 9" (20 cm x 22.5 cm) brown treasure chest so it overlaps one inch. Secure the lid to the chest by placing a brass fastener along the left side.

3. Glue the tissue puffs and foil across the top of the treasure chest to make jewels.

4. Add sequins and glitter.

Follow-Up Activities

Jewel Search

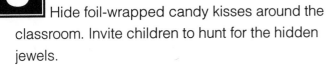

Hide foil-wrapped candy kisses around the classroom. Invite children to hunt for the hidden jewels.

Jewels, Jewels, Who Has the Jewels?

Invite children to sit in a circle. Have one child stand outside the room or cover his or her eyes for a few moments while you give a large jewel (inexpensive toy ring) to one child sitting in the circle. All children, including the child with the jewel, hold out their clasped hands in front of them as if they are holding a jewel. The child who was standing outside now comes to the circle and has three guesses to try to name who is actually holding the jewel.

Jewels Galore

Provide a collection of jewelry catalogs for children to browse. Help children learn the names and colors of the gems.

itchen • La Cocina

Materials (for each child)

- 12" x 18" (30 cm x 45 cm) any color construction paper
- magazines
- scissors
- glue

Directions

1. Invite children to cut out magazine pictures of objects, appliances, or utensils they would find in a kitchen.

2. Encourage children to glue their pictures on a piece of construction paper to create a kitchen scene.

Follow-Up Activities

Kitchen Contents

Read *My Kitchen* by Harlow Rockwell (New York: Greenwillow Books, 1980). This simple book is full of everyday objects that even the youngest children will recognize. Objects include milk (la leche), bread (el pan), spoon (la cuchara), table (la mesa), napkin (la servilleta), sink (el fregadero), pot (el pote), and stove (la estufa).

Kitchen Cabinets

Play a memory game with items found in kitchen cabinets. The first child says, "In my kitchen cabinet, I have (blank)." The next child repeats the sentence and then adds another item. The third child repeats what the two children previously have said and adds a third item. The game continues with the kitchen cabinet list getting longer and longer. Pictures of the kitchen cabinet objects will be especially helpful for ESL students.

Kitchen Corner

Set up a dramatic play area with kitchen tools and empty food boxes and packages. Invite children to prepare meals and bake their favorite desserts.

K ite • **La Cometa**

Materials (for each child)

- 9" x 12" (22.5 cm x 30 cm) any color construction paper for kite
- 1" (2.5 cm) squares of tissue in a variety of colors
- three 1" x 24" (2.5 cm x 60 cm) any color strips of tissue
- paintbrush
- 24" (60 cm) piece of yarn

Directions

1. Paint the kite with liquid starch.

2. Layer the various colored tissue squares on the wet starch.

3. Use the starch to attach the three 1" x 24" (2.5 cm x 60 cm) strips of tissue to the kite for the tail.

4. Allow the kite to dry overnight.

5. Punch a hole in the top of the kite and tie the yarn through the hole.

6. Have fun flying the kite!

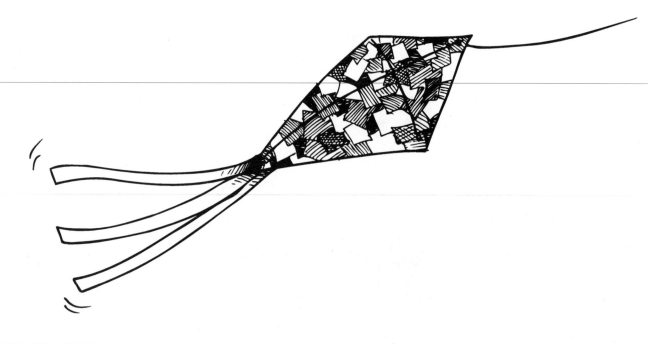

Follow-Up Activities

ite Song

Teach children the song, "Let's Go Fly a Kite."

Kite Power

Read *Gilberto and the Wind* by Marie Hall Ets (New York: Viking Press, 1963). In this story, Gilberto and his friend, the wind, spend the day having fun together. This book is also available in Spanish—*Gilberto y el Viento*.

Kite Flyers

Invite children to imagine what it would be like to sail up into the sky by holding the tail of a kite. Encourage children to describe their imaginary adventures and draw pictures to illustrate their stories.

 **emon • El Limón**

Materials (for each child)

- construction paper
  12" (30 cm) green square for tree top
  3" x 18" (7.5 cm x 45 cm) brown for tree trunk
- ten 1" x 2" (2.5 cm x 5 cm) yellow tissue paper for lemons
- glue
- scissors

Directions

1. Tear around the edges of the green square to make the tree top.

2. Tear along the long edges of the brown construction paper to make the tree trunk.

3. Glue the tree trunk to the top of the tree.

4. Round off all corners of the pieces of yellow tissues to make lemons.

5. Glue the lemons to the tree.

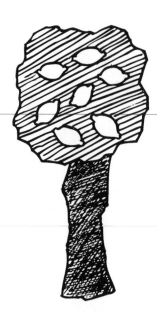

Follow-Up Activities

Looking at Lemons

Compare the size, shape, and number of seeds in a collection of lemons. Challenge children to estimate the circumference of a lemon by cutting a piece of string or yarn the length they think is needed to go around the fattest part of the lemon. Have children test their predictions.

Lemon Prints

Cut several lemons in half. Invite children to dip the lemons in paint and press them on construction paper to make lemon print designs.

Luscious Lemonade

Cut lemons in half and provide several juicers so each child can have an opportunity to squeeze the juice from a lemon. Add water, sugar, and ice to the freshly squeezed juice to make a refreshing drink.

# **L**ion • El León

Materials (for each child)

- 18" x 24" (45 cm x 60 cm) newsprint
- tempera paint
  light tan
  dark brown
  black
- tissue paper
  five 1" x 6" (2.5 cm x 15 cm) brown for mane
  five 1" x 6" (2.5 cm x 15 cm) gold for mane
  five 1" x 6" (2.5 cm x 15 cm) yellow for mane
- paintbrush
- crayons or markers

Directions

1. Paint a lion's face on the newsprint using the tan, brown, and black paint.

2. Place the tissue paper strips around the lion's head, alternating colors, to make the mane. Place one end of each tissue strip in the wet paint on the lion's face to make it stick.

3. Using a crayon or marker, write *lion* or *el león* under the lion's head.

Follow-Up Activities

Lion Lesson

Read *Dandelion* by Don Freeman (New York: Viking Press, 1964). In this story, a lion discovers the value of just being himself rather than trying to be something he is not.

Learn About Lions

Share some interesting facts about lions with your students. Newborn lions weigh only three or four pounds. Lions live in a group called a pride. It takes a lion about two years to become a successful hunter.

Lazy Lions

Invite children to walk, stretch, and yawn like lazy lions. Encourage children to dramatize other animals and invite the class to guess what animal they are.

Magic • La Magia

Materials (for each child)

- construction paper
  4" x 5" (10 cm x 12.5 cm) white for rabbit body
  3" (7.5 cm) white square for rabbit head
  two 1 1/2" x 3" (3.75 cm x 7.5 cm) white for rabbit ears
  3" x 15" (7.5 cm x 37.5 cm) black for hat brim
  8" x 9" (20 cm x 22.5 cm) black for hat
- pink and black crayons or markers
- brass fastener
- scissors
- glue

Directions

1. Round off the corners of the 4" x 5" (10 cm x 12.5 cm) piece of white construction paper to make the rabbit body.

2. Round off the 3" (7.5 cm) square of white construction paper to make the rabbit head.

3. Glue the rabbit head to the body.

4. Cut off two corners on each 1 1/2" x 3" (3.75 cm x 7.5 cm) piece of white construction paper to make two pointed rabbit ears.

5. Glue the ears to the top of the rabbit's head.

6. Using a pink crayon or marker, color the inside of the rabbit's ears.

7. Using a black crayon or marker, draw eyes, a nose, whiskers, and a mouth on the rabbit's face.

8. Glue the 3" x 15" (7.5 cm x 37.5 cm) black strip to the 8" x 9" (20 cm x 22.5 cm) piece of black construction paper to make the hat.

9. Fasten the bottom of the rabbit body to the brim of the upside down hat with a brass fastener.

Follow-Up Activities

Marvelous Magic Tricks

Teach the class a simple magic trick. For example, place a few raisins in a clear, plastic cup. Fill the cup with carbonated water. The raisins will move up and down in the glass magically!

Magic Lessons

Read *Strega Nona's Magic Lessons* by Tomie DePaola (San Diego: Harcourt Brace Jovanovich, 1982). In this story, Big Anthony disguises himself so he can take magic lessons from Strega Nona.

More Magic

Ray Broekel's *Now You See It* (Boston: Little, Brown, 1979) is a well-illustrated book of simple magic tricks for beginners. Many of the tricks can be done by young children.

ountains • Las Montañas

Materials (for each child)

- construction paper
  12" x 18" (30 cm x 45 cm) brown for mountains
  12" x 18" (30 cm x 45 cm) blue for background
- two large cotton balls
- fifteen 2" (5 cm) green tissue paper squares for trees
- chalk
- scissors
- glue

Directions

1. Draw a large *M* with chalk on the 12" x 18" (30 cm x 45 cm) piece of brown construction paper.

2. Cut on the line to make two mountain peaks.

3. Glue the mountains to the blue background.

4. Cut two corners off each 2" (5 cm) square of green tissue to make triangles.

5. Glue triangles in vertical rows of three to make trees on the mountain.

6. Spread the cotton balls and glue them to the top of the mountain peaks or in the sky to make clouds.

Follow-Up Activities

Mountain Movers

Read *Ming Lo Moves the Mountain* by Arnold Lobel (New York: Greenwillow, 1982). In this story, Ming Lo and his wife live in a house at the bottom of a large mountain. They love their house but not the mountain, so Ming Lo's wife decides Ming Lo should move it.

Mountain Camping

Invite children to use blocks to create a mountain in the dramatic play center. Encourage children to pretend they are camping in the mountains.

Mountain Music

Teach children the song, "The Bear Went Over the Mountain."

 est • El Nido

Materials (for each child)

- construction paper
  9" x 12" (22.5 cm x 30 cm) blue for background
  ten 1/4" x 4" (6 mm x 10 cm) brown, gold, tan, or beige for twigs
  four 1 1/2" x 3" (3.75 cm x 7.5 cm) white for eggs
- crayons or markers
- scissors
- glue

Directions

1. Draw a smile on the 9" x 12" (22.5 cm x 30 cm) piece of blue construction paper as an outline for the nest.

2. Build the nest by gluing the 1/4" x 4" (6 mm x 10 cm) strips of construction paper above the smile outline.

3. Round off the corners of the four 1 1/2" x 3" (3.75 cm x 7.5 cm) pieces of white construction paper to make four eggs.

4. Glue the eggs in the nest.

5. Using crayons or markers, write *nest* or *el nido*.

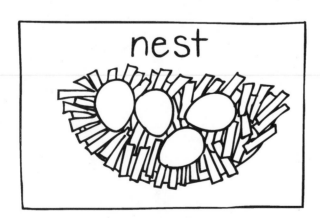

Follow-Up Activities

Neat Nests

Melt 1/4 cup (62.5 mL) butter and 6 cups (1.5 L) miniature marshmallows. Combine the melted marshmallows with 6 cups (1.5 L) corn flakes. Give each child a small portion of the mixture on a sheet of waxed paper. Invite children to mold the sticky corn flakes into a nest and add some jelly bean eggs. (Makes 30 nests.)

Nests for Napping

Read *Who Took the Farmer's Hat* by Joan L. Nodset (New York: Harper & Row, 1963). In this delightful story, the wind sweeps the farmer's hat away. He asks each animal if they know where it is. The farmer finally discovers that Bird has turned it into a nice round brown nest.

Nests Are Homes

Remind children that nests are homes for birds. Encourage children to make a list of other animal homes.

Night • La Noche

Materials (for each child)

- construction paper
  12" x 18" (30 cm x 45 cm) black for background
  scraps of gold, olive green, grey, brown, or tan
- chalk
- foil stars
- scissors
- glue

Directions

1. Cut the scraps of construction paper to make a picture of something at night and glue them to the black background.

2. Place a moon and foil stars in the night sky.

3. Write the word *night* or *la noche* on the picture.

Follow-Up Activities

Nocturnal Animals

Read *Night Animals* by Millicent Ellis Selsam (New York: Four Winds Press, 1979). The beautiful illustrations in this book provide an interesting look at nocturnal creatures.

Now I Lay Me Down to Sleep

Read *Goodnight Moon* by Margaret Wise Brown (New York: Harper Collins, 1991). Encourage children to talk about their favorite bedtime stories or nightime rituals.

Night Sky

Invite children to observe the moon once a week for a month. Have them draw a picture of what they see at each observation. Help each child glue the four pictures on one large sheet of construction paper.

cean • El Océano

Materials (for each child)

- construction paper
  12" x 18" (30 cm x 45 cm) white for background
  several 2" x 3" (5 cm x 7.5 cm) pieces in various colors for fish
- tissue paper
  several 1" (2.5 cm) blue and green squares for water
  six 1/4" x 3" (6 mm x 7.5 cm) green for seaweed
- liquid starch
- paintbrush
- crayons or markers
- scissors
- glue

Directions

1. Paint the 12" x 18" (30 cm x 45 cm) sheet of white construction paper with liquid starch.

2. Place layers of 1" (2.5 cm) squares of blue and green tissue over the entire sheet of white paper.

3. Paint starch over the tissues to blend the colors.

4. Add 1/4" x 3" (6 mm x 7.5 cm) strips of green tissue vertically to make seaweed.

5. Cut ovals and triangles from 2" x 3" (5 cm x 7.5 cm) pieces of construction paper to make fish.

6. Using crayons or markers, add details to the fish.

7. Glue the fish in the ocean.

Follow-Up Activities

Odd Octopus

Read *I Was all Thumbs* by Bernard Waber (Boston: Houghton Mifflin, 1975). In this story, an octopus that was once held captive by a research scientist is set free and finds dealing with the natural ocean environment quite an adjustment.

On Top and Under

Ask children to brainstorm a list of things that swim, float, or glide on top of the ocean and things that are found deep under the ocean. Begin by asking children to sort the following into those two categories and then adding to the lists with their own ideas—scuba diver (el buceador), submarine (el submarino), dolphin (el delfín), shark (el tiburón), sand (la arena), seaweed (el alga marina), and fishing line (el hilo de pescar).

Only Some Float

Encourage children to experiment with objects that sink and float. Provide a tub of water and various objects. Invite children to make predictions before they test each object's buoyancy.

Octagons and Ovals • Los Octágonos y Los Óvalos

Materials (for each child)

- construction paper
  9" x 12" (22.5 cm x 30 cm) black for background
  scraps in various sizes and colors
- octagon and oval patterns
- white chalk
- scissors
- glue

Directions

1. Trace several octagons and ovals in various sizes and colors.

2. Glue the shapes on the black construction paper to make an interesting design.

3. Using white chalk, write *octagons and ovals* or *los octágonos y los óvalos* on the black background.

Follow-Up Activities

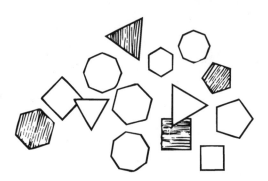

Octagons and Others

Display a triangle, square, pentagon, hexagon, and octagon. Discuss the differences in the shapes and invite children to count the number of sides each shape has.

Oval Arrangement

Challenge children to cut pictures from magazines of oval-shaped objects. Children might find pictures of such items as an egg, face, necklace pendant, picture frame, balloon, or grape. Display the pictures on a bulletin board.

Octagon Patterns

Give each child an octagon pattern. Invite children to trace the pattern eight times on a large sheet of construction paper to make an interesting design.

Pineapple • La Piña

Materials (for each child)

- construction paper
  6" x 9" (15 cm x 22.5 cm) brown
  9" x 12" (22.5 cm x 30 cm) white with pineapple outline drawn on it
- six 1" x 4" (2.5 cm x 10 cm) strips of green tissue paper
- crayons or markers
- glue

Directions

1. Tear the brown construction paper into small pieces.

2. Glue the brown pieces of paper on the pineapple outline.

3. Glue the green tissue paper strips to the top of the pineapple.

4. Using crayons or markers write *pineapple* or *la piña*.

Follow-Up Activities

Picking Pineapples

Make a pineapple-shaped deck of ten cards. Write a different number, letter, word, or shape on the back of five of the cards. Repeat with the other five cards to make matching pairs. Place all the cards face down. Invite children to pick two pineapples and turn them over to try to make a match.

Pineapple Tasting

Invite children to taste both fresh and canned pineapple. Ask them to describe the differences and similarities. Explain to children that fruit and vegetables are canned so they will last longer without spoiling.

Pineapple Growing

Place the top of a pineapple in potting soil. Invite children to water and watch it grow.

Puppy • **El Perrito**

Materials (for each child)

- construction paper
  5 1/2" x 8 1/2" (13.75 cm x 21.25 cm) dark brown for body
  6" (15 cm) dark brown square for head
  two 3" x 6" (7.5 cm x 15 cm) light brown for ears
  1 1/2" x 6" (3.75 cm x 15 cm) dark brown for tail
  2" x 8" (5 cm x 20 cm) black for eyes, nose, mouth and spots
- paper lunch bag
- scissors
- glue
- pencil

Directions

1. Glue 5 1/2" x 8 1/2" (13.75 cm x 21.25 cm) piece of brown construction paper to the paper bag, fitting it up under the flap.

2. Round off all corners of the 6" (15 cm) square of dark brown construction paper to make a head.

3. Glue the head to the bag flap.

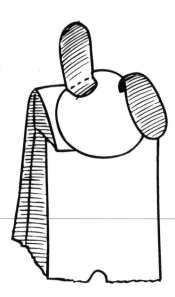

4. Round off all corners of the 3" x 6" (7.5 cm x 15 cm) pieces of light brown construction paper to make two ears.

5. Fold over a small flap at the top of each ear. Glue the ear flaps to the top of the head and flop the ears forward.

6. Round one end of the 1 1/2" x 6" (3.75 cm x 15 cm) dark brown piece of construction paper to make a tail.

7. Curl the tail by wrapping it around a pencil.

8. Glue the tail to the back of the bag.

9. Cut eyes, nose, mouth and spots from the 2" x 8" (5 cm x 20 cm) piece of black construction paper. Glue them to the puppy.

Follow-Up Activities

Playful Puppy

Read *Follow That Puppy!* by Brian Mangas (New York: Simon & Schuster, 1991). In this story, a playful puppy pulls his owner under the bushes, through the flowers, and across the stream, until the leash finally breaks with a snap! A daring chase begins as the little dog takes off for a frisky and frolicsome adventure.

Pets Galore

Invite each child to draw a picture of a pet they own or would like to own. Combine the pictures in a class book.

Pet Parade

Encourage children to bring in a favorite stuffed animal from home. Children who do not own a stuffed animal can make one by stuffing and decorating a paper bag. Have a pet parade.

Quiet • Quedo

Materials (for each child)

- construction paper
  4" (10 cm) pink or brown square for hand
  1" x 3" (2.5 cm x 7.5 cm) pink or brown for finger
  9" x 12" (22.5 cm x 30 cm) white for background
- tempera paint
- paintbrush
- crayons or markers
- brass fastener
- glue

Directions

1. Paint a head and shoulders on the 9" x 12" (22.5 cm x 30 cm) piece of white paper.

2. After the paint has dried, cut the outline out.

3. Using crayons or markers, add facial features.

4. Round off all corners of the 4" (10 cm) square of pink or brown construction paper to make a hand.

5. Round off the top two corners of the 1" x 3" (2.5 cm x 7.5 cm) piece of pink or brown construction paper to make an extended index finger.

6. Glue the finger to the top of the hand.

7. Using the brass fastener, attach the hand just below the chin of the painted head.

8. Move the hand back and forth to say, "Shh! Be quiet."

Follow-Up Activities

Quiet Listening

Invite children to sit quietly for three minutes without making a sound. Encourage them to listen closely. After the quiet time is up, ask children to name the sounds they heard.

Quiet Riot

Read Virginia Sicotte's *A Riot of Quiet* (New York: Holt, 1969). This is a wonderful book of various things that make sounds of silence such as bubbles bursting. Children might like to try replicating some of these silent sounds.

Quiet Sounds

Read *Quiet* by Peter Parnall (New York: Morrow, 1989). In this story, a child lies quietly on the ground waiting for animals to come near.

Quintuplets • Los Quintillizos

Materials (for each child)

- construction paper
  five 2" x 3" (5 cm x 7.5 cm) various colors for finger puppets
  five 1 1/2" (3.75 cm) pink or brown squares for heads
- finger puppet pattern
- scissors
- crayons or markers
- glue

Directions

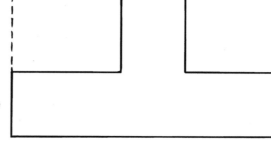

1. Trace around the finger puppet pattern on each 2" x 3" (5 cm x 7.5 cm) piece of construction paper.

2. Cut the finger puppets out.

3. Round off the corners of the five 1 1/2" (3.75 cm) squares to make heads.

4. Glue a head on each finger puppet.

5. Using crayons or markers, add details to each puppet face so that the puppets look identical.

6. Fold each finger puppet base to make a ring and glue the tabs in place.

7. Place one finger puppet on each finger with the faces on the palm side of your hand.

Bilingual ABC's © 1995 Fearon Teacher Aids

Follow-Up Activities

Quick Five

Invite children to make sets of five by finding five identical objects around the classroom. For example, children could make a set of five books, five pieces of chalk, five paper clips, five pencils, or five shoes.

Quesadilla Cuts

Make quesadillas by grilling grated cheese between tortillas. Give each group of five children a quesadilla and challenge the children to divide the tortilla into five equal parts before enjoying their treat.

Quilts Five by Five

Give each child a 5" (12.5 cm) square of construction paper to decorate with crayons or markers. Help children place the squares in groups five across and five down to create patchwork quilts.

Refrigerator • El Refrigerador

Materials (for each child)

- 12" x 18" (30 cm x 45 cm) white construction paper
- magazines
- scissors
- crayons or markers
- glue

Directions

1. Fold the 12" x 18" (30 cm x 45 cm) piece of white construction paper in half to make a 9" x 12" (22.5 cm x 30 cm) refrigerator.

2. Make the doors for the refrigerator and freezer by cutting across the top flap (about 1/3 from the top) to the fold.

3. Using crayons or markers, draw door handles.

4. Cut pictures of food from magazines.

5. Glue the food pictures inside the refrigerator.

6. Write the word *refrigerator* or *el refrigerador*.

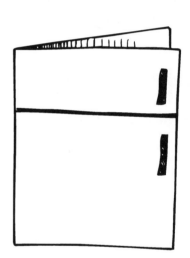

Follow-Up Activities

Refrigerated Foods

Invite the class to make a list of their favorite foods. Challenge children to divide the list of foods into three groups—foods that need refrigeration, foods that are kept in the freezer, and foods that sit on a shelf in the cupboard.

Refrigerator Relay

Divide the class into teams. Place ten food pictures cut from magazines in front of each team. Place a large piece of butcher paper, cut to look like a refrigerator, on the wall in front of each team. On a given signal, challenge the teams to quickly decide which foods belong in the refrigerator and to place them on the wall.

Rustic Refrigerators

Invite students to think of ways food could be kept cold without using a refrigerator. Explain to students the principle of the ice box which was commonly used before refrigerators were available.

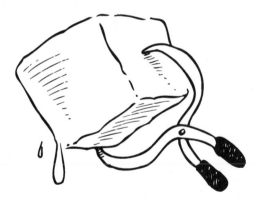

Ruler • La Regla

Materials (for each child)

- 2" x 12" (5 cm x 30 cm) heavy cardboard ruled with inch or centimeter marks
- crayons or markers

Directions

1. Using a crayon or marker, trace over the ruler marks.

2. Write the appropriate number underneath each mark.

3. Using crayons or markers, decorate the backside of the ruler.

Follow-Up Activities

R uler Height

Invite children to estimate how many of their rulers it would take to equal their height. Measure each child's height and mark it on a strip of paper hanging on a wall.

R ugs, Raincoats, and Rectangles

Invite children to measure objects around the room that begin with the letter R. Children can use their rulers to measure a rubber band (la cinta de goma), rubber stamp (el sello de goma), raincoat (el impermeable), rectangle (el rectángulo), rock (la piedra), or the rug (la alfombra).

R estaurant "Rulers"

Ask children if they can think of anything that can not be measured using a ruler. Show children some tools that are used to measure liquid and are often used in cooking (measuring spoons and measuring cups). Place the liquid measuring tools at a water table and invite children to practice measuring.

Sit • Sientase

Materials (for each child)

- construction paper
  1" x 3" (2.5 cm x 7.5 cm) brown for shoe
  2" x 9" (5 cm x 22.5 cm) blue for leg
  3" x 6" (7.5 cm x 15 cm) green for shirt
  1 1/2" x 6" (3.75 cm x 15 cm) green for sleeve
  2" (5 cm) pink or brown square for head
  1" (2.5 cm) pink or brown square for neck
  1 1/2" (3.75 cm) pink or brown square for hand
- two brass fasteners
- crayons or markers
- scissors
- glue

Directions

1. Round off one corner of the 1" x 3" (2.5 cm x 7.5 cm) piece of brown construction paper to make a shoe.

2. Glue the shoe to one end of the 2" x 9" (5 cm x 22.5 cm) blue leg.

3. Round off all four corners of the 3" x 6" (7.5 cm x 15 cm) piece of green construction paper to make the shirt.

4. Use a brass fastener to attach the leg to the bottom of the shirt.

5. Round off the corners of the 1 1/2" (3.75 cm) square of pink or brown construction paper to make a round hand.

6. Glue the hand to the end of the 1 1/2" x 6" (3.75 cm x 15 cm) green sleeve.

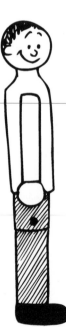

7. Glue the sleeve to the shirt about one inch from the top.

8. Round off the corners of the 2" (5 cm) square of pink or brown construction paper to make a head.

9. Glue the head to the 1" (2.5 cm) square neck.

10. Using crayons or markers, add hair and facial features to the head.

11. Cut the leg at the knee and reattach it with a brass fastener.

Follow-Up Activities

Simon Says

Give children commands that begin with the letter S as you play "Simon Says." For example, Simon can ask children to skip, sit, slide, spin, squirm, ski, or stand.

Skip, Slither, Slink, Sit

Place placards with the letter S on them around the floor of the room or play area. Play music while children skip, slither, slink, or do any other action that begins with the letter S. When the music stops, invite children to find a letter S and sit on it.

Seat Options

Encourage children to make a list of different types of chairs and other things they sit on. The list might include a rocking chair, sofa, stool, horse, pillow, bench, and bleachers.

nake • La Serpiente

Materials (for each child)

- red pipe cleaner
- six 2" x 6" (5 cm x 15 cm) strips of various colored tissue

Directions

1. Thread the multi-colored tissue strips onto the pipe cleaner, weaving them in and out. Push the strips together to gather them.

2. Leave a bit of red pipe cleaner showing at one end to be the snake's tongue.

3. Bend the snake into an "S" shape.

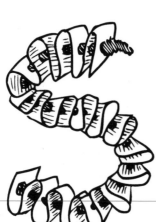

Follow-Up Activities

Snake Line

Invite children to play "Follow the Leader" by making a long snake line. Each child puts his or her hands on the waist of the child in front. The lead child initiates movement for the others to follow as they slither around the play area.

Snake's Mistake

Read *The Snake's Mistake* by Keith Faulkner and Jonathon Lambert (Los Angeles: Price Stern Sloan, 1988). This clever story is presented in poetic verse with an unusual and interesting page design. The snake's mistake becomes apparent as he encounters a young girl who uses a pepper shaker as a means of saving her friends who have become the snake's snack.

Snake Snack

Read "I'm Being Swallowed by a Boa Constrictor" in Shel Silverstein's *Where the Sidewalk Ends* (New York: Harper & Row, 1974).

Taxi and Tunnel
• El Taxi y El Túnel

Materials (for each child)

- construction paper
  6" x 18" (15 cm x 45 cm) black for road
  9" x 18" (22.5 cm x 45 cm) brown or gray for tunnel
  3" x 4" (7.5 cm x 10 cm) yellow for taxi
- black crayon or marker
- yellow or white chalk
- scissors
- glue

Directions

1. Make a road by drawing a dotted line down the center of the 6" x 18" (15 cm x 45 cm) piece of black construction paper.

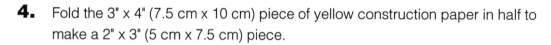

2. Fold over a 1/2" (1.25 cm) flap on each 18" (45 cm) side of the piece of brown or gray construction paper to make a tunnel.

3. Glue one flap of the tunnel underneath the road. Arch the tunnel over the road and glue the other flap in place.

4. Fold the 3" x 4" (7.5 cm x 10 cm) piece of yellow construction paper in half to make a 2" x 3" (5 cm x 7.5 cm) piece.

5. Draw a taxi on the folded yellow paper with the top of the taxi running along the fold.

6. Cut out the taxi leaving it attached at the fold.

7. Using a black crayon or marker, draw doors and tires.

8. Write the word *taxi* or *el taxi* on the car.

9. Children can drive their taxis through the tunnel.

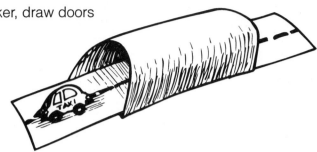

Follow-Up Activities

Tunnel Travel

Help children make a tunnel by placing a group of tables or desks together. Invite children to travel through their homemade tunnel.

Transportation Types

Taxis are one form of transportation. Encourage children to use construction paper scraps to make other types of transportation such as a train (el tren), bicycle (la bicicleta), skateboard (la tabla de patines), truck (el camión), and motorcycle (la motocicleta). Glue the paper vehicles to a large sheet of butcher paper to make a mural.

Taxi Ride

Help children build a taxi in the dramatic play center using chairs and blocks. Invite children to take turns playing the role of taxi drivers and passengers.

urtle • La Tortuga

Materials (for each child)

- construction paper
  6" x 8" (15 cm x 20 cm) dark green for body
  5" x 7" (12.5 cm x 17.5 cm) dark green for back tube
  3" x 12" (7.5 cm x 30 cm) light green for head and tail
  2" x 8" (5 cm x 20 cm) light green for feet
  4" x 8" (10 cm x 20 cm) light green for spots
- crayons or markers
- scissors
- glue

Directions

1. Round off the corners on the 6" x 8" (15 cm x 20 cm) piece of dark green construction paper to make a turtle body.

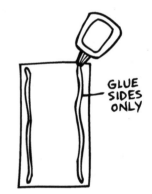

GLUE SIDES ONLY

2. Place a line of glue down each 7" (17.5 cm) side of the the 5" x 7" (12.5 cm x 17.5 cm) piece of dark green construction paper. Glue it the center back of the turtle body.

3. Round off the corners of one end of the 3" x 12" (7.5 cm x 30 cm) piece of light green construction paper to make a head. Cut the other end of this piece to a point to make the tail.

4. Cut the 2" x 8" (5 cm x 20 cm) light green paper into 2" (5 cm) squares to make four feet.

5. Round off the corners on each foot.

6. Glue the four feet to the body in the appropriate places.

7. Cut circles from the 4" x 8" (10 cm x 20 cm) piece of light green construction paper to make spots.

8. Glue the spots on the turtle's back.

9. When the glue on the back of the turtle is dry, slip the head and tail piece through the opening.

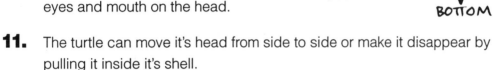

TOP

BOTTOM

10. Using crayons or markers, draw the eyes and mouth on the head.

11. The turtle can move it's head from side to side or make it disappear by pulling it inside it's shell.

12. Write the word *turtle* or *la tortuga*.

Follow-Up Activities

Tortoise and the Hare

After reading the well-known story of the lazy hare and the persistent tortoise, invite children to create skits to retell the story.

Turtle and the Moon

Read *The Turtle and the Moon* by Charles Turner (New York: Dutton, 1991). This gentle story is about a wistful and lonely turtle who benefits from the mysteries of the moonlight.

Turtle Trivia

Encourage children to share what they know about turtles including how they look, what they eat, and where they live.

Uniform • El Uniforme

Materials (for each child)

- construction paper
  9" x 12" (22.5 cm x 30 cm) blue for shirt
  two 3" (7.5 cm) yellow squares for epaulets
- two 2" x 3" (5 cm x 7.5 cm) pieces of yellow tissue for epaulet fringe
- three 3" (7.5 cm) strips of red or yellow roving for braid on jacket front
- six 1" (2.5 cm) squares of aluminum foil for buttons
- four 2" (5 cm) strips of red or yellow roving for braid on sleeves
- star stickers
- scissors
- glue

Directions

Before children begin working, draw a 3" (7.5 cm) cutting line 2" (5 cm) from the top on each side of the 9" x 12" (22.5 cm x 30 cm) piece of blue construction paper.

Draw an 8" (20 cm) cutting line on each side of the paper starting from the bottom of the paper and 2" (5 cm) in from each side.

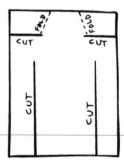

1. Cut on the lines to make the sleeves and collar.

2. Fold the collar in to the center of the paper and glue it in place.

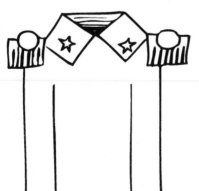

3. Add foil stars to the collar.

4. Fringe the edge of each 2" x 3" (5 cm x 7.5 cm) piece of yellow tissue.

5. Glue yellow fringe to each shoulder on the 9" x 12" (22.5 cm x 30 cm) blue construction paper.

6. Round the corners of the 3" (7.5 cm) squares of yellow construction paper.

7. Glue a yellow circle on top of the fringe on each shoulder to make epaulets.

8. Glue the three 3" (7.5 cm) strips of red or yellow roving across the front of the uniform.

9. Round the corners of the aluminum foil squares to make shiny buttons.

10. Glue the foil circles on each end of the roving.

11. Glue the two 2" (5 cm) strips of red or yellow roving on the end of each sleeve.

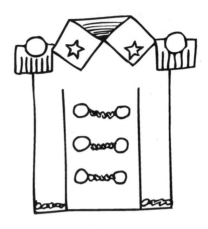

Follow-Up Activities

U nusual Outfits

Invite children to brainstorm a list of unusual or unique uniforms they have seen people wear. Challenge children to explain why they think some jobs or organizations require uniforms and others do not.

U niform Steps

Explain to children that the word uniform also refers to exact precision such as when a marching band or drill team make their steps uniform or exactly alike. Challenge children to work in small groups to choreograph a simple set of uniform steps that they can perform together.

U niform Design

Read *Drummer Hoff* by Ed Emberley (New York: Simon & Schuster, 1967). Invite children to compare and contrast the features of each military figure's uniform (private, corporal, sergeant, captain, major, general).

Unique • Único

Materials (for each child)

- butcher paper as long as the child is tall
- pencil
- tempera paint
- crayons or markers

Directions

Before children begin working, have each child lie down on his or her sheet of butcher paper as you draw around the child's body.

1. Using paint, crayons, and markers, add clothes, hair, facial features, and other details to make a giant paper copy of yourself.

2. Think about ways you are different from anyone else in your class.

3. Write "I'm unique because . . ." or "Soy único porque . . . ."

Follow-Up Activities

Unique Gifts

Encourage each child to share a favorite toy or gift that he or she thinks has some unique quality. Invite children to talk about how it is unique.

Uniquely You

Describe a child by telling about his or her unique attributes without using the child's name. Challenge the class to guess who is being described.

Unicorns and Unicycles

Remind children that the word *unique* means one of a kind. Other words that start with "uni" also mean "one." A unicorn has one horn and a unicycle has one wheel. Invite children to recite the alphabet or a poem they all know in unison—as if they were one voice.

Violets • Las Violetas

Materials (for each child)

- construction paper
  6" (15 cm) purple square for vase
  12" x 18" (30 cm x 45 cm) yellow for background
- twenty 1" (2.5 cm) squares of purple tissue for violets
- 6" (15 cm) piece of roving
- green tempera paint in shallow pan
- clothespin
- scissors
- glue

Directions

1. Fold the 6" (15 cm) square of purple construction paper in half.

2. Cut an "S" shape on the open side to make a vase.

3. Open the vase and glue it near the bottom of the 12" x 18" (30 cm x 45 cm) piece of yellow construction paper.

4. Clip the piece of roving to the clothespin. Holding the clothespin, dip the roving into the green paint and then lay it on the yellow background paper several times to make stem prints.

5. Crumple up each 1" (2.5 cm) square of purple tissue to make violets.

6. Glue the violets to the stems.

Follow-Up Activities

Vases of Fragrance

Provide several small "vases" of fragrance for students to identify. Opaque film canisters make great "vases." Punch several small holes in the lid of each canister. Fill the canisters with items such as vanilla, cinnamon, vinegar, or mouthwash. Challenge students to smell the fragrances and identify them.

Violet Village

Invite each child to make a drawing or painting of a village in which everything is violet. Encourage children to talk about their illustrations.

Very Violet

Provide a collection of various shades of violet paint swatches (available in paint stores). Invite children to experiment with different amounts of red, blue, and white paint to recreate the shades of violet represented by the paint swatches.

olcano • El Volcán

Materials (for each child)

- 12" (30 cm) square of brown construction paper for mountain
- three 6" (15 cm) squares of tissue paper — one each of yellow, red, and orange
- liquid starch and orange tempera paint mixed in a squeeze bottle

Directions

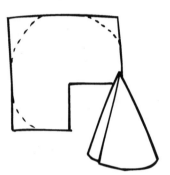

1. Cut a one quarter slice out of the 12" (30 cm) square of brown construction paper.

2. Round the corners of the remaining piece of brown construction paper and glue it into a cone shape to make a mountain.

3. Cut 1/2" (1.25 cm) off the top of the mountain cone.

4. Cut fringe along one edge of the tissue squares stopping each cut 1" (2.5 cm) from the edge.

5. Roll the three colors of fringed tissue together and stick them into the top of the mountain cone so the fringed ends plume out of the top of the mountain.

6. Drip the paint mixture down the sides of the mountain to represent lava.

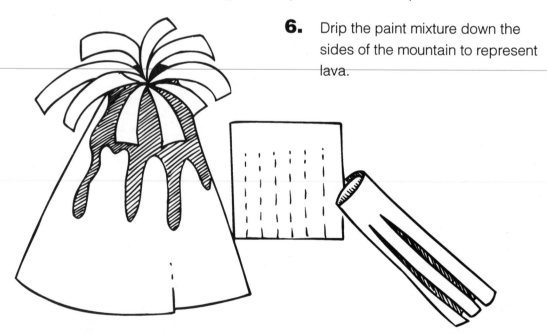

Follow-Up Activities

Volcano Eruptions

Give each child a piece of waxed paper and a small paper cup. Have children place the paper cup upside down on the waxed paper to represent a mountain. Have each child place a spoonful of baking soda on top of the paper cup mountain, add vinegar to the baking soda, and watch it foam and run down the mountainside.

Volcano Viewing

Collect pictures of volcanoes from a source such as *National Geographic* magazine. Bind the pictures together to make a volcano picture book. Place the book at a center for children to enjoy.

Volcano Reports

Read *Hill of Fire* by Thomas P. Lewis (New York: Harper & Row, 1971). This I-Can-Read story is based upon reports of the eruption of a volcano in Mexico.

atermelon • La Sandía

Materials (for each child)

- 12" x 18" (30 cm x 45 cm) white construction paper
- tissue paper
    - 1" (2.5 cm) green squares for rind
    - 1" (2.5 cm) white squares for rind
    - 1" (2.5 cm) red squares for watermelon
    - 1" (2.5 cm) black squares for seeds
- black crayon or marker
- liquid starch
- paintbrush
- glue

Directions

1. Using a black crayon or marker, draw a big smile across the bottom of the white construction paper.

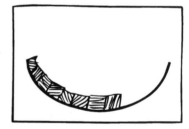

2. Place a row of green tissue squares along the smile line and paint over them with liquid starch to make them stick.

3. Place row of white tissue squares above the row of the green tissue and paint them with liquid starch.

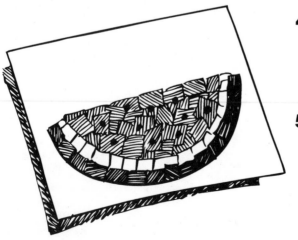

4. Fill in the rest of the watermelon with red tissue squares and paint over them with liquid starch.

5. Roll the black tissue squares into tiny balls and glue them on the red part of the watermelon to look like seeds.

Follow-Up Activities

Watermelon Lover

Read *Greedy Greeny* by Jack Gantos (New York: Doubleday, 1979). In this story, a little monster disobeys his mother by eating the family watermelon. He reaps the consequences of his greed in a dream.

Which Melon?

Provide a variety of melons for children to taste such as watermelon, cantaloupe, and honeydew. Make a class graph to show the children's preferences.

Watermelon Seeds

Invite children to categorize fruit by the amount of seeds it has. For example, some fruits have only one seed (peach, plum) and others have many seeds (watermelon, apple, orange, cantaloupe).

indow • La Ventana

Materials (for each child)

- construction paper
  12" x 18" (30 cm x 45 cm) blue for window
  2" x 18" (5 cm x 45 cm) brown strip for wooden pane
  2" x 12" (5 cm x 30 cm) brown strip for wooden pane
- two 4" x 12" (10 cm x 30 cm) any color tissue paper for curtains
- 2" x 24" (5 cm x 60 cm) any color tissue paper for valance
- crayons or markers
- glue

Directions

1. Form a cross with the brown strips of construction paper and glue them to the 12" x 18" (30 cm x 45 cm) piece of blue construction paper to make window panes.

2. Pleat the tops of the tissue curtains and glue them on each side of the window.

3. Pleat the 2" x 24" (5 cm x 60 cm) valance and glue it to the top of the window.

4. Using crayons or markers, draw a picture of what can be seen outside the window.

Follow-Up Activities

Window Ways

Encourage children to pantomime washing windows while singing, "This is the way we wash the windows, wash the windows, wash the windows. This is the way we wash the windows, so early in the morning." Children can add other verses such as "This is the way we open the window . . . ," "This is the way we close the window . . . ," or "This is the way we look out the window . . ." and add appropriate actions.

Window Wall

Transform one wall of your classroom into a huge window, creating cross bars with construction paper and using tissue paper to make curtains on each side. Invite children to make various items to place in the window to make it look as if they were looking through it.

Window Watch

Invite children to play a word memory game. The first child begins by saying, "Out of my window I can see . . . ." Each child repeats the sentence the last child said and adds a new word.

-ray • Los Rayos X

Materials (for each child)

- construction paper
  6" (15 cm) pink or brown square for head
  6" x 9" (15 cm x 22.5 cm) black for x-ray
- white tempera paint in a shallow pan
- cotton swabs
- crayons or markers
- scissors
- glue

Directions

1. Round off the corners of the 6" (15 cm) square of pink or brown construction paper to make a head.

2. Using crayons or markers, add hair and facial features to the head.

3. Glue the head to the top of the 6" x 9" (15 cm x 22.5 cm) piece of black construction paper.

4. Using a cotton swab dipped in white tempera paint, draw a spine and ribs on the black x-ray film.

Follow-Up Activities

X-ray Examination

If possible, collect some x-ray film from a local doctor's office to show the children what an actual x-ray looks like. Challenge children to explain how x-rays help doctors and patients.

X-ray Eyes

Place a box, with an object inside it, in front of the room. Ask children to pretend they have x-ray vision that allows them to see inside the box without opening it. Invite children to make a guess about what they think is inside the box. Encourage them to make reasonable guesses by considering the size of the box. After all guesses have been made, open the box.

X-ray Technician

Explain to children what an x-ray technician does when he or she goes to work. Discuss what type of training and knowledge the job might require.

ylophone • El Xilófono

Materials (for each child)

- construction paper
  2" x 18" (5 cm x 45 cm) black for xylophone base
  1" x 10" (2.5 cm x 25 cm) red for bar
  1" x 9" (2.5 cm x 22.5 cm) orange for bar
  1" x 8" (2.5 cm x 20 cm) yellow for bar
  1" x 7" (2.5 cm x 17.5 cm) green for bar
  1" x 6" (2.5 cm x 15 cm) blue for bar
  1" x 5" (2.5 cm x 12.5 cm) purple for bar
  1" x 4" (2.5 cm x 10 cm) pink for bar
  1" x 3" (2.5 cm x 7.5 cm) gray for bar
  1/2" x 10" (1.25 cm x 25 cm) brown for mallet
  2" (5 cm) black square for end of mallet
- glue

Directions

1. Glue the colorful bars to the 2" x 18" (5 cm x 45 cm) piece of black construction paper. Begin with the longest bar (red) and glue the bars in order of size, ending with the shortest (gray).

2. Round off the corners of the 2" (5 cm) square of black construction paper.

3. Glue the black circle to the end of the 1/2" x 10" (1.25 cm x 25 cm) brown mallet.

4. Glue the mallet to the xylophone.

Follow-Up Activities

Xylophone Sounds

Fill three glasses with different amounts of colored water. Invite children to tap each glass gently with a spoon and compare the sounds they hear. Challenge children to play a simple tune.

X-citing Sounds

Challenge children to create other sounds using materials found in the classroom. For example, children could create a rhythm by tapping their pencils on a desktop.

X-cellent Orchestra

Invite children to combine xylophone sounds and other musical rhythms they have discovered how to make to create an orchestra.

Y ard • La Yarda

Materials (for each child)

- 12" x 18" (30 cm x 45 cm) white construction paper
- thin green and blue tempera paint
- paintbrush
- crayons or markers

Directions

1. Use thin green paint to create a light wash at the bottom of the 12" x 18" (30 cm x 45 cm) piece of white construction paper.

2. Use the thin blue paint to create a sky at the top of the white construction paper.

3. After the paint is dry, use crayons or markers to add details to the yard.

Follow-Up Activities

Yard Collages

Invite children to tour the play area at school and collect twigs, leaves, and small pebbles. Encourage children to glue their yard objects to construction paper to make yard collages.

Yard Map

Challenge children to make a map of their play yard at home, the play yard at school, or the play area at a nearby park.

Yard Cover

Give each child a small milk carton with the top cut off. Help children fill the cartons with potting soil and sprinkle grass seed on top. Encourage children to water their mini grass-covered yards and watch them grow.

Yolk • La Yema

Materials (for each child)

- construction paper
    9" (22.5 cm) any color square for plate
    6" (15 cm) white square for egg white
- 12" (30 cm) strip of yellow roving for yolk
- crayons or markers
- scissors
- glue

Directions

1. Round the corners of the 9" (22.5 cm) square of construction paper to make a round plate.

2. Decorate the border of the plate using crayons or markers.

3. Tear around the outside of the 6" (15 cm) square of white construction paper to make the irregular form of an egg white.

4. Place a small amount of glue in the center of the egg white.

5. Coil the yellow roving on the glue to form the yolk.

6. Glue the egg to the center of the plate.

Follow-Up Activities

Yolk Comparisons

Compare the yolks of raw, soft-boiled, and hard-boiled eggs. Challenge children to describe the differences.

Yummy Yolks

Ask children to name different ways eggs can be prepared (scrambled, fried, poached, hard-boiled). Make a graph to show children's preferences.

Yikes!

Read Mother Goose's "Humpty Dumpty." Challenge children to think of ways they could protect an egg from breaking if it fell off a wall.

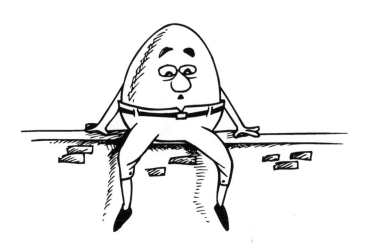

ig Zag • Zig Zag

Materials (for each child)

- construction paper
  12" x 18" (30 cm x 45 cm) any color
  ten 1/2" x 3" (1.25 cm x 7.5 cm) various colored strips
- glue

Directions

1. Make zig zag patterns by placing the strips of construction paper on the 12" x 18" (30 cm x 45 cm) sheet of construction paper.

2. Glue the strips in place.

Follow-Up Activities

Zig Zag Road

Challenge children to use large blocks to make a giant zig zag road.

Zigging and Zagging

Encourage children to play "Follow the Leader" and move in a zig zag pattern around the play area.

Zig Zag Mouse

Read Sally Noll's *Watch Where You Go* (New York: Greenwillow, 1990). A gray mouse's zig zag journey through what appears to be the grass, rocks, and tree branches of the forest proves his mother's adage that "things are not always what they seem."

oo • El Zoológico

Materials (for class)

- large sheet of butcher paper
- tempera paint (various colors)
- construction paper (various colors)
- paintbrushes
- sponges
- clothespins
- scissors
- glue

Directions

Place the large sheet of butcher paper on the floor or attach it to a wall low enough so children have easy access to it.

1. Dip paintbrushes or sponges attached to clothespins in paint. Spread the paint on the large butcher paper to create a zoo background.

2. Paint zoo animals on pieces of construction paper.

3. When the paint is dry, cut the animals out.

4. Glue the animals to the zoo background to make a class mural.

Follow-Up Activities

Zoo in the Room

Invite each child to pantomine his or her favorite zoo animal while his or her classmates guess what animal it is.

Zoo Train

Read *1,2,3 to the Zoo* by Eric Carle (New York: Philomel, 1982). In this counting story, each train car has one more zoo animal than the car before it.

Zebras and More!

Read Tana Hoban's *A Children's Zoo* (New York: Greenwillow, 1990). This book is full of excellent photographs of a variety of zoo animals.

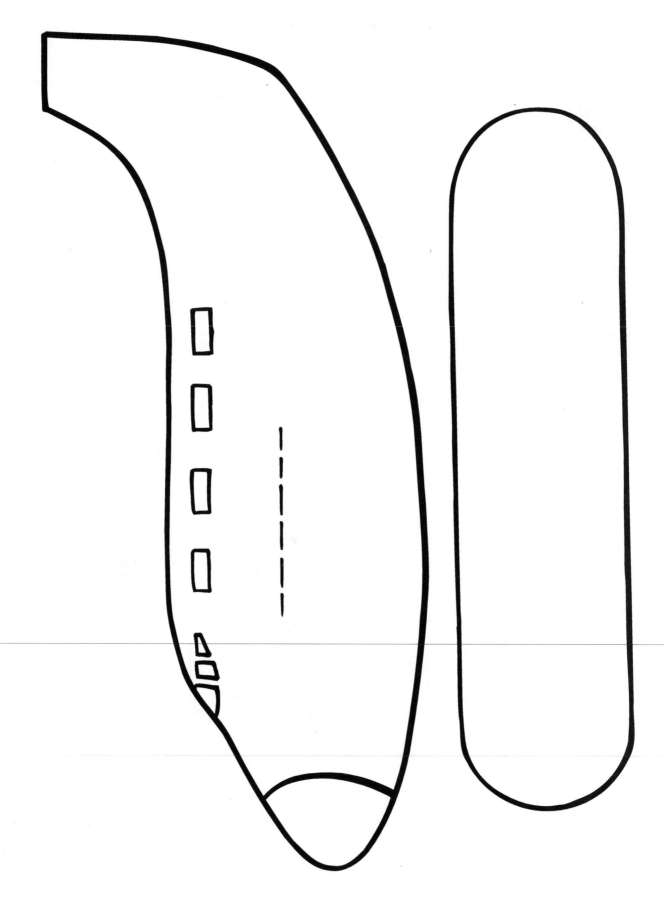

Spanish Pronunciation Guide

el acróbata (el ah-**kro**-bah-tah), acrobat

el actor (el ahk-**tor**), actor

la actriz (lah ahk-**trees**), actress

la alfombra (lah ahl-**fom**-brah), rug

el alga marina (el **ahl**-gah mah-**ree**-nah), seaweed

la arena (lah ah-**ray**-nah), sand

el arquero (el ar-**kay**-ro), archer

la arquitecta (lah ar-kee-**tek**-tah), architect

la artista (lah ar-**tees**-tah), artist

el astronauta (el ahs-tro-**now**-tah), astronaut

el astrónomo (el ahs-**tro**-no-mo), astronomer

el atleta (el aht-**lay**-tah), athlete

el avión (el ah-**byon**), airplane

la barba (lah **bar**-bah), beard

el barco y la ballena (el **bar**-ko ee lah bah-**yay**-nah), boat and whale

la bicicleta (lah bee-see-**klay**-tah), bicycle

el buceador (el boo-say-ah-**dor**), scuba diver

el camión (el kah-**myon**), truck

el castillo (el kahs-**tee**-yo), castle

la cinta de goma (lah **seen**-tah day **go**-mah), rubber band

el coche (el **ko**-chay), car

la cocina (lah ko-**see**-nah), kitchen

la cometa (lah ko-**may**-tah), kite

la cuchara (lah koo-**chah**-rah), spoon

el delfín (el del-**feen**), dolphin

el dinosaurio (el dee-no-**sow**-ryo), dinosaur

el doctor (el dahk-**tor**), doctor

el elefante (el ay-lay-**fahn**-tay), elephant

el ejercicio (el eh-her-**see**-see-oh), exercise

la estufa (lah es-**too**-fah), stove

las flores (lahs **flo**-res), flowers

la fregadero (el fray-gah-**day**-ro), sink

la fruta (lah **froo**-tah), fruit

el garaje (el gah-**rah**-hay), garage

el ganso (el **gahn**-so), goose

el hilo de pescar (el **ee**-lo day pes-**kar**), fishing line

el hipopótamo (el ee-po-**po**-tah-mo), hippopotamus

hola (**oh**-lah), hello

el impermeable (el eem-per-may-**ah**-blay), raincoat

el insecto (el een-**sek**-to), insect

la isla (lah **ees**-lah), island

la jalea (lah **lay**-ah), jelly

las joyas (lahs **ho**-yahs), jewels

la leche (lah **lay**-chay), milk

el león (el **lay**-on), lion

el limón (el lee-**mon**), lemon

la magia (lah mah-**he**-ah), magic

la mesa (lah **may**-sah), table

las montañas (lahs mon-**tah**-nyahs), mountains

la motocicleta (lah mo-to-see-**klay**-tah), motorcycle

el nido (el **nee**-do), nest

la noche (lah **no**-chay), night

el océano (el o-**say**-ah-no), ocean

el pan (el pahn), bread

la piedra (lah **pyay**-drah), rock

la piña (la **pee**-nyah), pineapple

porque (por-**kay**), because

el pote (el **po**-tay), pot

la princesa (lah preen-**say**-sah), princess

el príncipe (el **preen**-see-pay), prince

el puente levadizo (el **pwen**-tay lay-bah-**dee**-so), drawbridge

el perrito (el pair-**rree**-toh), puppy

quedo (kay-**doh**), quiet

los quintillizos (los keen-tee-**yee**-sos), quintuplets

los rayos x (los **rrah**-yos **ay**-kees), x-ray

el rectángulo (el rrek-**tan**-goo-lo), rectangle

el refrigerador (el ray free-hay-rah-**door**), refrigerator

la regla (lah **rray**-glah), ruler

la reina (lah **rray**-nah), queen

el rey (el rray), king

la sandía (lah sahn-**dee**-uh), watermelon

el sello de goma (el **say**-yo day **go**-mah), rubber stamp

la serpiente (lah ser-**pyen**-tay), snake

la servilleta (lah ser-bee-**yay**-tah), napkin

sientase (see-**en**-tah-say), sit

el submarino (el soob-mah-**ree**-no), submarine

la tabla de patines (lah **tah**-blah day pah-**tee**-nes), skateboard

el taxi y el túnel (el **tah**-gsee ee el **too**-nel), taxi and tunnel

el tiburón (el tee-boo-**ron**), shark

la tortuga (lah tor-**too**-gah), turtle

el tren (el tren), train

el trono (el **tro**-no), throne

único (oo-**nee**-koh), unique

el uniforme (el oo-nee-**for**-may), uniform

la ventana (lah ben-**tah**-nah), window

las violetas (las vee-oh-**lay**-tahs), violets

el volcán (el bol-**kahn**), volcano

el xilófono (el see-**lo**-fo-no), xylophone

la yarda (lah **yar**-dah), yard

la yema (lah **yay**-mah), yolk

el zoológico (el so-o-**lo**-hee-ko), zoo